AF228364

History in Pictures

FOCUS ON
THE GREAT DEPRESSION

Elliott Smith

Lerner Publications ◆ Minneapolis

LETTER FROM CICELY LEWIS

Dear Reader,

Imagine being in an argument with a classmate and the teacher asks what happened. Your classmate tells their version of the story, but you don't get to share your version. Do you think this is fair? Well, this is what has happened throughout history.

This series looks at different events in US history with a focus on photos that help tell stories of people from underrepresented groups.

I started the Read Woke challenge in response to the needs of my students. I wanted my students to read books that challenged social norms and shared perspectives from underrepresented and oppressed groups. I created Read Woke Books because I want you to be knowledgeable and compassionate citizens.

As you look through these books, think about the photos that have captured history. Why are they important? What do they teach you? I hope you learn from these books and get inspired to make our world a better place for all.

Yours in solidarity,

—Cicely Lewis, Executive Editor

TABLE OF CONTENTS

Think critically about the photos throughout this book. Who is taking the photos and why? What is their viewpoint? Who are the people in the photos? What do these photos tell us?

Many of the photos in this book were taken to advertise the US's New Deal program. The government paid photographers to show what life in the US was like and gain support for the New Deal programs.

Unemployed people line up outside of a soup kitchen during the Great Depression.

SOUP SAVES

THE **G**REAT **D**EPRESSION WAS A MAJOR ECONOMIC CRASH THAT HIT THE US IN THE LATE 1920S. Many photos from this period show people waiting in line for soup. During the Great Depression, soup kitchens sprang up across the country. They were critical in ensuring that people survived this rough stretch.

Why soup? Commonly made with potatoes and other vegetables, soup was easy to produce in massive quantities.

Soup kitchens often added water to the soup so the supply wouldn't run out.

Lines stretched around blocks. Some kitchens were set up in churches with long tables to seat the maximum number of people. Other kitchens had no seating areas. People would bring their own metal buckets, and workers ladled soup to go.

Most soup kitchens operated from donations, but donations were hard to come by as the Great Depression continued to hurt the US economy. In 1932 the government gave $4 million (a little over $80 million in today's money) for states to open more soup kitchens.

Before the Great Depression hit, the economy had been growing.

Schoolchildren receive a meal in 1930.

In the 1920s, girls play and dance in New York City.

CHAPTER 1
THE GREAT DEPRESSION

THROUGHOUT MOST OF THE 1920S, THE US ECONOMY WAS BOOMING. This period became known as the Roaring Twenties. Rich people bought cars and furniture, partied, and invested in the stock market. But many people of color and women didn't get to share in the wealth. And the era ended abruptly on October 29, 1929, with a stock market crash. A market crash is a rapid and often unanticipated drop in how much American companies are worth. The economic fall would last for about ten years. It remains the longest and most severe depression experienced in modern history.

Economic experts have several theories behind the stock market crash. One was that a decline in spending by people led to a decline in production by manufacturers. Another is that the rapid rise of the stock market in the 1920s wasn't sustainable. People began selling stocks, and the market bottomed out. The stock market would eventually fall 90 percent.

In 1939 two men sit and talk in Oklahoma.

More than fifteen million people became unemployed
during the Depression. Thousands of banks failed. Numerous
companies went out of business. Many people lost their
homes or access to a safe place to live and were forced to
build makeshift towns.

President Herbert Hoover miscalculated the seriousness of
the Depression. He predicted it would be over in sixty days.
Hoover also believed that the government should not provide
any relief to those most affected. Once a well-liked president,
Hoover became less popular.

The US was not the only nation to be hit hard by the Great
Depression. The entire world dealt with economic struggles.
International trade fell sharply. Countries could not afford to
purchase important materials, products, and crops.

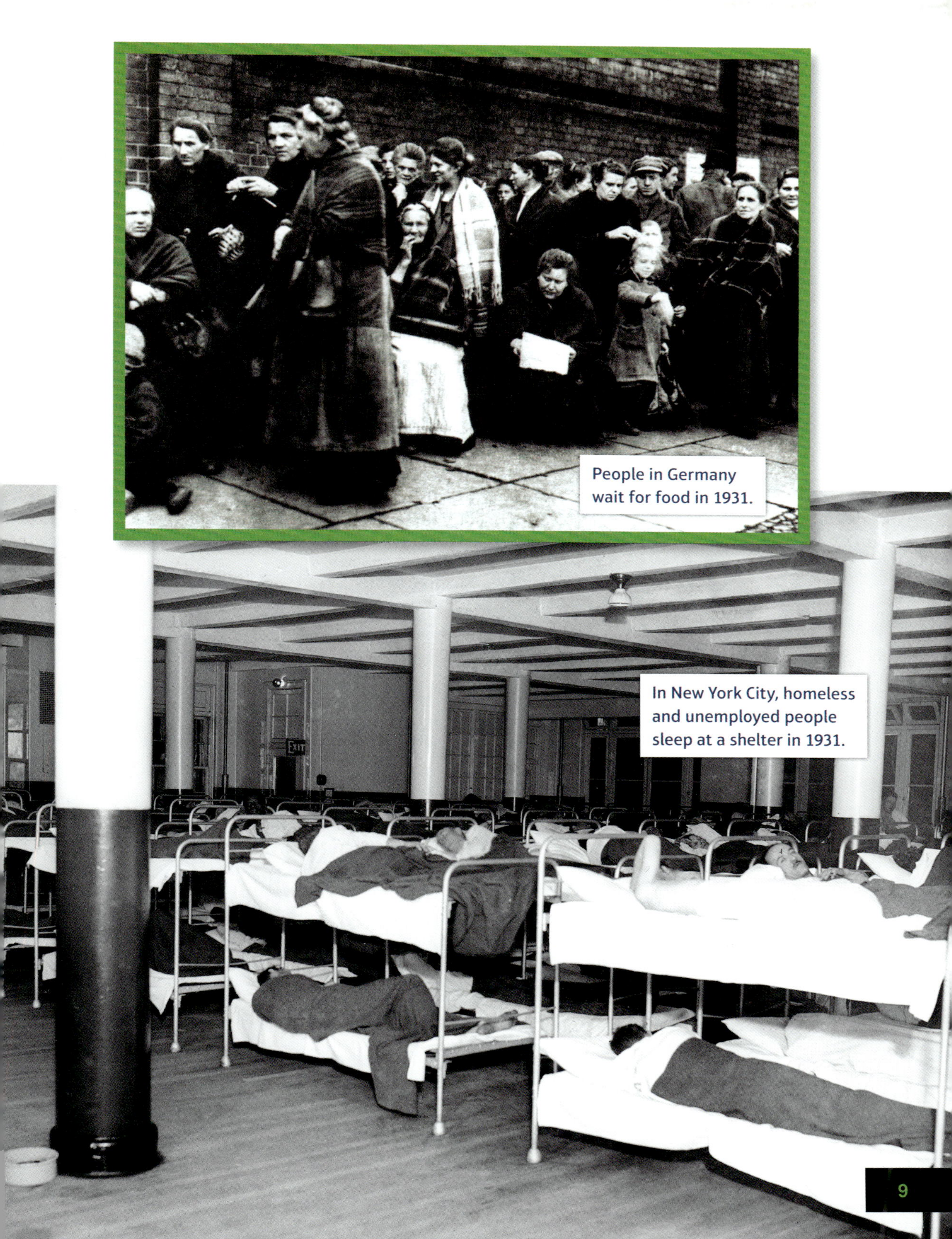

People in Germany
wait for food in 1931.

In New York City, homeless
and unemployed people
sleep at a shelter in 1931.

CHAPTER 2
THE DUST BOWL

AGRICULTURE WAS HIT HARD DURING THE GREAT DEPRESSION. Farmers saw the price of their crops fall to record lows. Many farms were lost altogether, as families couldn't afford to keep them and banks foreclosed on the land.

As prices fell, farmers turned to desperate measures. Some began to burn corn on their farms for heat rather than coal since corn was cheaper. At times, the air smelled like popcorn because of all the corn burning.

Then, in 1934, excessive heat broiled the Midwest. Crops could not survive the conditions. The following year, severe winds began to blow across the Plains. Altogether, around twenty states were affected by the Dust Bowl (1930–1936) and droughts.

The Dust Bowl was created from new farming methods that stressed the soil while overproducing crops. The blowing dust made crops hard to grow, and the prices increased.

CULTURAL IMPACT

Dorothea Lange's *Migrant Mother* photograph (*facing page*) became an iconic image of the Depression-era struggle. Lange was able to travel across the US and take photos because of a government program. The photographer captured the picture of Florence Owens Thompson and her children in 1936 and created a story about Thompson. Later, Thompson told her own story. The photograph made Thompson famous for being poor, but she was never paid as a model.

REFLECT

Do you think it should be allowed to take photos of people who are suffering and spread these images? Why or why not?

A family stands with their harvest in 1938. The Dust Bowl made harvests smaller than usual.

With no other choice, many farmers began migrating west. The journey was rough, and there was little promise of a better life. More than four hundred thousand people left the Plains during the Dust Bowl.

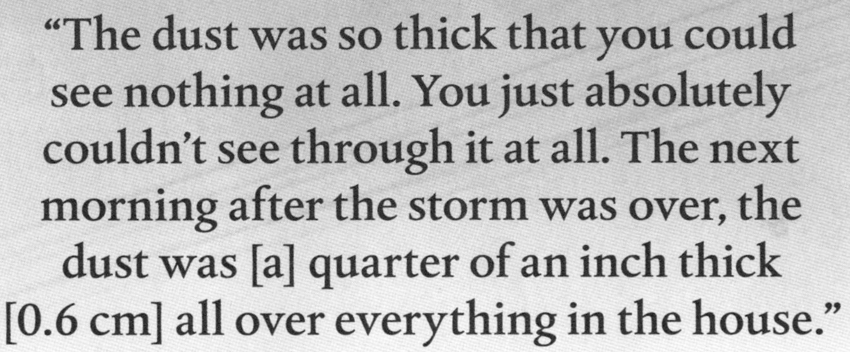

"The dust was so thick that you could see nothing at all. You just absolutely couldn't see through it at all. The next morning after the storm was over, the dust was [a] quarter of an inch thick [0.6 cm] all over everything in the house."

—CHARLIE SPURLOCK,
recorded in 1940 at a migrant camp

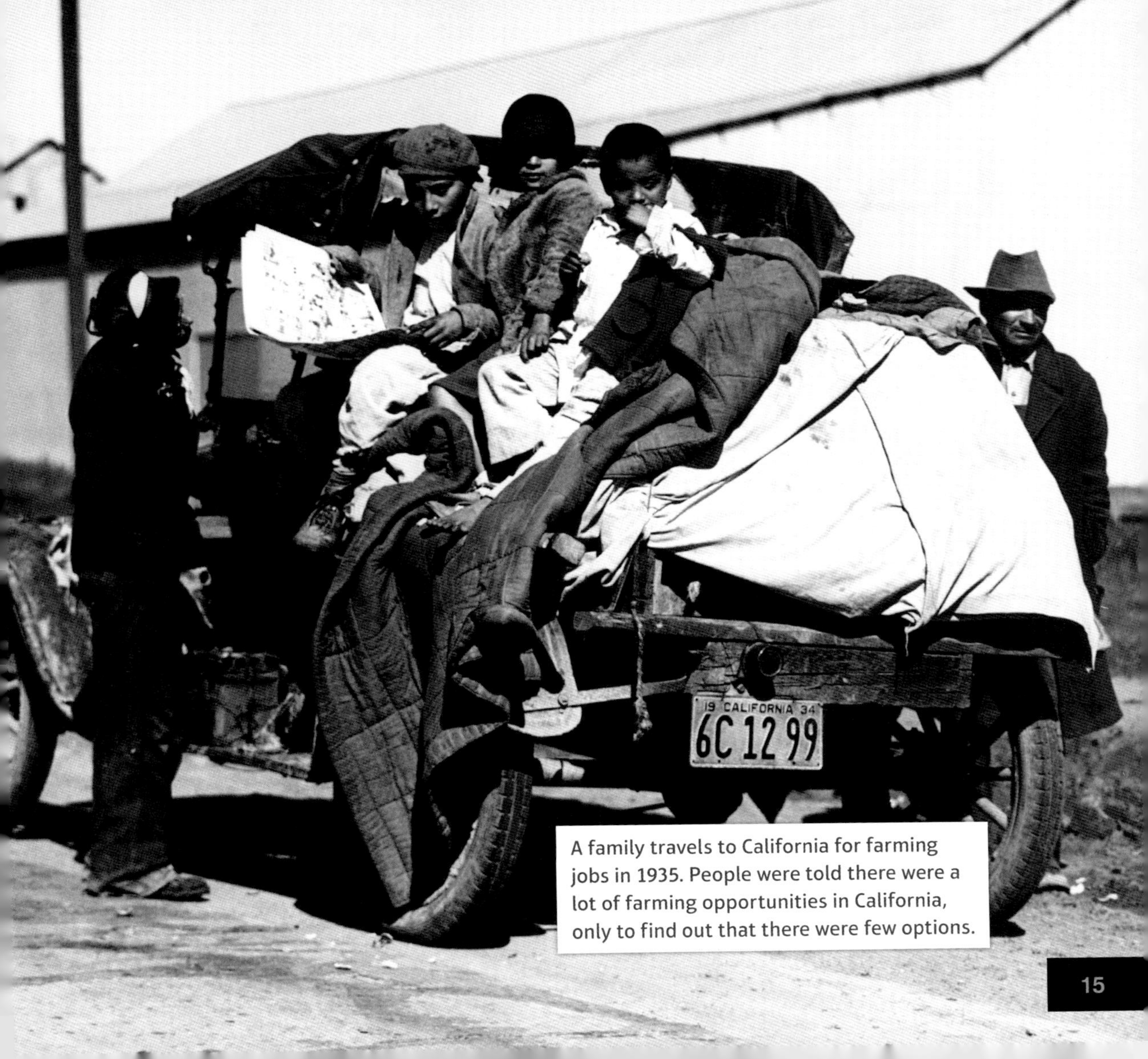

A family travels to California for farming jobs in 1935. People were told there were a lot of farming opportunities in California, only to find out that there were few options.

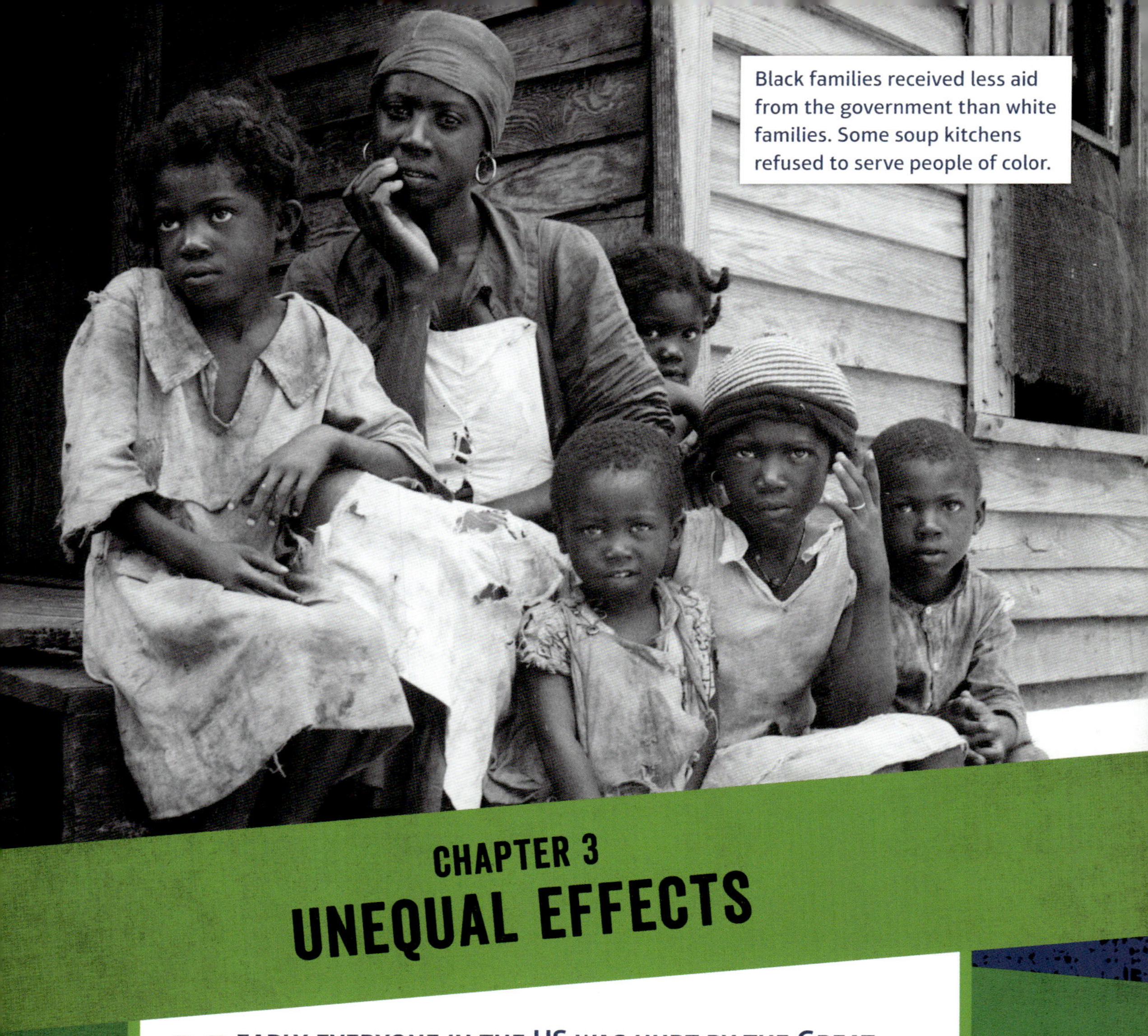

CHAPTER 3

UNEQUAL EFFECTS

NEARLY EVERYONE IN THE US WAS HURT BY THE GREAT DEPRESSION. But it hit Black Americans the hardest. They suffered the highest rate of unemployment during the 1930s. And since many Black people had low-paying jobs, they had little-to-no savings to help them survive the crash. People who worked on farms or in other people's homes were not protected by federal law, so employers could pay Black people less than white people without consequence.

The saying went that Black people were "last hired, first fired." The numbers agree. By 1932 the unemployment rate for Black people was nearly 50 percent. In places like Atlanta, nearly 70 percent of Black people were without work. Those numbers were nearly double or triple the rate of white unemployment.

Black families who worked on farms or as sharecroppers fell into debt or were forced off their land. This played a part

Some Black people boycotted, or refused to shop at, places that only hired white people.

"In the Depression, the men could not get jobs, and especially the black men. Here was my father with a degree in chemistry, and he could not get a job."

—WANDA BRIDGEFORTH,
a Chicago resident during the Depression

in the Great Migration (1916–1970), when Black residents moved from the rural South to cities, the North, or outside of the US after the Depression. It was also a time of economic uncertainty, job loss, and racial violence.

Women's employment numbers rose in the Depression. Employers paid women less than men. They often only hired women who were young, white, and unmarried, while women of color lost their jobs.

A group of people migrating north for new job opportunities in 1940

Black voters wait to cast their ballot in 1925.

CHAPTER 4
A NEW DEAL

THE PRESIDENTIAL ELECTION OF 1932 WAS A TURNING POINT IN THE GREAT DEPRESSION. Franklin D. Roosevelt promised a "New Deal" for the country, and he won the election in a landslide. He was supported by many Black voters. A lot of them voted for a Democrat for the first time.

The New Deal created government agencies to fight the Depression. Programs provided relief to those most in need. Some programs helped thousands regain employment while addressing other needs. Roads, bridges, highways, airports, and national parks were built, often by workers who had lost their jobs.

In 1935 FDR created a Second New Deal. It included even more agencies and aid. The Social Security Act was passed. This ensured pensions for millions of Americans, though it did not cover the majority of Black people at the time. This program and several other New Deal programs still exist. And food banks are used to help millions of people.

Despite being supported by Black voters, FDR signs the Social Security Act, which excluded a lot of Black people.

IMPACTFUL IMAGES

Gordon Parks was a famous Black artist who captured the lives of Black Americans. He wanted to travel the US as Dorothea Lange did to take her *Migrant Mother* photo. But Parks was excluded from the program because of his race. Later, he met Ella Watson, part of the cleaning crew at the office where he worked. She showed Parks around Washington, DC. Parks took several important pictures, including this one of Watson at work, titled *Washington, DC, Government Charwoman* (*facing page*).

While the New Deal didn't end the Great Depression or stop the unemployment crisis, it is still considered a success. It expanded the role of the federal government. Most important, it gave people hope.

The event that marked the end of the Great Depression was an unfortunate one. The attack on Pearl Harbor in December 1941 brought the US into World War II (1939–1945). The war effort boosted nearly every industry, increased employment, and lifted the economy.

In 2020 the market crashed with the spread of COVID-19. Many people lost their jobs or had to stay home to take care of their children. Again, women and people of color were hit the hardest. The US has faced dark events in its history and is still confronting its past. But people continue to educate one another and work to create a more equitable future.

TAKE ACTION

Learn more about the Great Depression, and find out how to get involved. Here are some ways to get started:

Learn more about the Green New Deal, and find out how you can support it at https://www.investopedia.com/the -green-new-deal-explained-4588463.

Discover how racial income inequality continues to affect people of color. Start a social justice club at your school to spread the word.

Ask an older adult if they have any recollections of the Great Depression.

Volunteer at a local food bank or start a food drive to help those who are hungry.

TIMELINE

1929 — The stock market crash on October 29 starts the Great Depression.

1930 — Banks begin to fail, leading to many people losing all their money and becoming homeless.

1931 — Soup kitchens begin appearing in major cities in the US.

1932 — On November 8 Franklin Delano Roosevelt wins the presidential election and promises a New Deal for the US.

1934 — On April 14 a huge dust storm blows across the Midwest, which becomes the Dust Bowl.

1936 — Photographer Dorothea Lange takes a photo of Florence Owens Thompson in March.

1941 — Japan attacks the US at Pearl Harbor on December 7. The US officially enters World War II several days later.

1942 — Gordon Parks photographs Ella Watson.

PHOTO REFLECTION

In 1935 Mary McLeod Bethune became the first Black woman to lead a US federal agency, the National Youth Administration's Office of Minority Affairs. She helped Black people find jobs during the Great Depression. Why is it important for all people to be represented in government?

Draw or write about a time when you weren't represented. How did it feel? What can you do to include people?

GLOSSARY

ECONOMY: the process or system by which goods and services are produced, sold, and bought in a country or region

FORECLOSE: to take property because the money owed for it has not been paid

ICONIC: a person or thing that is an object of respect or admiration

INVEST: to put up money in hopes of making a profit

MIGRANT: a person who travels from place to place to find work

PENSION: money paid at regular periods to a person who is retired

SHARECROPPER: a person who farms another person's land and shares what is produced. Landlords often kept tenants in debt so they could make more money off the tenants.

SUSTAINABLE: using resources in a way that they will be available for a long time

SOURCE NOTES

15 "WPA Recordings Captured Life History of 10,000 Everyday People," NPR, May 25, 2020, https://www.npr.org/2020/05/25/861819242/wpa-recordings-captured-life-history-of-10-000-everyday-people.

18 Neenah Ellis, "Survivors of the Great Depression Tell Their Stories," NPR, November 27, 2008, https://www.npr.org/templates/story/story.php?storyId=97468008.

READ WOKE READING LIST

Britannica: The Great Depression
https://kids.britannica.com/students/article/Great-Depression
/274639

Ducksters: The Great Depression
https://www.ducksters.com/history/us_1900s/great
_depression.php

Favreau, Marc. *Crash: The Great Depression and the Fall and Rise of America*. New York: Little, Brown, 2018.

Kiddle: Great Depression Facts for Kids
https://kids.kiddle.co/Great_Depression

Sandler, Martin W. *Picturing a Nation: The Great Depression's Finest Photographers Introduce America to Itself.* Somerville, MA: Candlewick, 2021.

Schwartz, Heather E. *The Great Depression and the New Deal*. Huntington Beach, CA: Teacher Created Materials, 2019.

Tyner, Dr. Artika R. *Focus on the Great Migration*. Minneapolis: Lerner Publications, 2023.

Weatherford, Carole Boston. *Gordon Parks: How the Photographer Captured Black and White America*. Chicago: Albert Whitman, 2015.

INDEX

PHOTO ACKNOWLEDGMENTS

National Archives (541927), p. 4; Library of Congress (LC-USZ62-101428, fsa-8a26000, 8b29289v, LC-USF34- 018241-C, LC-USF34- 009058-C, LC-USZ62-69109, fsa.8c35333), pp. 5, 7, 10, 11, 13, 15, 17, 18, 19; NY Daily News Archive/Getty Images, p. 6; AP Photo, pp. 8, 9 (bottom), 21; INTERFOTO/ Alamy Stock Photo, p. 9 (top); Bettmann Archive/Getty Images, p. 20; © Gordon Parks, p. 23; Vic Hinterlang/Shutterstock.com, p. 24; Cecily Lewis portrait photos by Fernando Decillis.

Cover image: Library of Congress (LC-DIG-fsa-8b29597).

Content consultant: Dr. Jennifer Jane Marshall

Lerner Publications Company
An imprint of Lerner Publishing Group, Inc.
241 First Avenue North
Minneapolis, MN 55401 USA

For reading levels and more information, look up this title at www.lernerbooks.com.

Main body text set in Aptifer Sans LT Pro.
Typeface provided by Linotype AG.

Designer: Emily Harris
Lerner team: Martha Kranes

Library of Congress Cataloging-in-Publication Data

Names: Smith, Elliott, 1976– author.
Title: Focus on the Great Depression / Elliott Smith.
Description: Minneapolis : Lerner Publications, [2023] | Series: History in pictures (read woke books) | Includes bibliographical references and index. | Audience: Ages 9–14 | Audience: Grades 4–6 | Summary: "The Great Depression uprooted many people's lives. Learn about racist policies that made the depression worse for Black Americans, the period's global impact, and lasting changes from the era"— Provided by publisher.
Identifiers: LCCN 2021045413 (print) | LCCN 2021045414 (ebook) | ISBN 9781728423470 (library binding) | ISBN 9781728462875 (paperback) | ISBN 9781728461403 (ebook)
Subjects: LCSH: Depressions—1929—United States—Juvenile literature. | United States—History—1933–1945—Juvenile literature. | New Deal, 1933–1939—Juvenile literature. | African Americans—Government policy—United States—History—20th century—Juvenile literature. | African Americans—United States—Social conditions—20th century—Juvenile literature. | African Americans—United States—Economic conditions—20th century—Juvenile literature.
Classification: LCC HB3717 1929 .S558 2022 (print) | LCC HB3717 1929 (ebook) | DDC 330.973/0916—dc23

LC record available at https://lccn.loc.gov/2021045413
LC ebook record available at https://lccn.loc.gov/2021045414

Manufactured in the United States of America
1-49185-49316-1/25/2022